NATIONS IN THE NEWS

Kazakhstan

By Charles Piddock

Academic Consultant: Jay Bergman
Professor of History
Central Connecticut State University
New Britain, Connecticut

WORLD ALMANAC® LIBRARY

Please visit our Web site at: www.garethstevens.com
For a free color catalog describing World Almanac® Library's list of high-quality books
and multimedia programs, call 1-800-848-2928 (USA) or 1-800-387-3178 (Canada).
World Almanac® Library's fax: (414) 332-3567

Library of Congress Catalog-in-Publication Data

Piddock, Charles.
   Kazakhstan / by Charles Piddock.
    p. cm. — (Nations in the news)
   Includes bibliographical references and index.
   ISBN-10: 0-8368-6708-4 — ISBN-13: 978-0-8368-6708-4 (lib. bdg.)
   ISBN-10: 0-8368-6715-7 — ISBN-13: 978-0-8368-6715-2 (softcover)
   1. Kazakhstan—History—Juvenile literature. I. Title.
 II. Series: Piddock, Charles. Nations in the news.
 DK908.6.P53   2007
 958.45—dc22   2006011215

First published in 2007 by
World Almanac® Library
A Member of the WRC Media Family of Companies
330 West Olive Street, Suite 100
Milwaukee, WI 53212 USA

A Creative Media Applications, Inc. Production
Design and Production: Alan Barnett, Inc.
Editor: Susan Madoff
Copy Editor: Laurie Lieb
Proofreader: Laurie Lieb and Donna Drybread
Indexer: Nara Wood
World Almanac® Library editorial direction: Mark J. Sachner
World Almanac® Library editor: Gini Holland
World Almanac® Library art direction: Tammy West
World Almanac® Library production: Jessica Morris

Cover photo: Shamil Zhumatov/Reuters/Landov

Photo credits: Associated Press: pages 5, 6, 19, 21, 23, 24, 25, 29, 33, 34, 35, 37, 38, 40; Getty Images: pages 8, 41;
Landov: pages 9, 26, 28, 30; The Bridgeman Art Library: pages 10, 11, 14; Northwind Pictures Archive: pages 12, 13;
The Granger Collection: page 16; Library of Congress: pages 17, 18; Foster and Partners: page 43; Maps courtesy of
Ortelius Design.

Printed in the United States of America

1 2 3 4 5 6 7 8 9 10 09 08 07 06

Table of Contents

Cover photo : A Kazakh oil worker walks along a newly-opened oil
pipeline at a railway station Atasu December 15, 2005.

Boom Time

"The year 2005 went down in the history of our country as a year that is worth outlining in gold," Nursultan Nazarbayev, the president of Kazakhstan, told his nation on New Year's Eve.

The president's words struck no one as hollow or false—at least as far as the economy was concerned. In 2005,

Kazakhstan extends over a vast area of Eurasia (the landmass composed of Europe and Asia) and borders Russia, China, Kyrgyzstan, Uzbekistan, and Turkmenistan. Its coastline is on the Caspian Sea. Although it is the ninth-largest country in the world, its sparsely populated, arid steppes make it only the fifty-seventh-largest country in the world by population.

Nursultan Nazarbayev

The man who has led Kazakhstan since independence has been called a dictator, a "modern-day Sultan of the Steppes," and "the father of his nation." Nursultan Nazarbayev (*shown left*) is perhaps all those things—and more.

Nazarbayev, a soft-spoken man in his late sixties, comes from very humble beginnings. He was born in 1940 in a village in southwestern Kazakhstan. His parents were shepherds. After high school, he worked at a steel plant in the town of Temirtau in northern Kazakhstan. He joined the Communist Youth League and worked his way up the ranks of the Communist Party. By the time he left northern Kazakhstan in 1980 for the then capital city of Almaty (still Kazakhstan's largest city), he was well on his way to the top post in Kazakhstan's Communist Party, which he attained in 1989. In 1991, when the Soviet Union dissolved, he was the natural choice to lead an independent Kazakhstan. A **referendum** in 1995 extended Nazarbayev's term in office. In 1999, he won another seven-year term as president. In 2005, he won a third term.

To his supporters, Nazarbayev is the man who has led the nation to prosperity and kept peace between Kazakhstan's **ethnic** groups. To his opponents, he is a dictator who has concentrated power and wealth in the hands of his family and supporters. In 2000, Nazarbayev pushed through laws granting him a powerful role in Kazakhstan even when he leaves office.

Kazakhstan's economy grew by more than 9 percent (compared to 3.5 percent growth for the U.S. economy), giving the nation's economy an astounding 75 percent growth in the last seven years alone. More people had more money than ever before. Trade boomed and new construction could be seen everywhere. New highways, oil pipelines, rail lines, apartment houses, and government buildings seemed to rise up in Kazakhstan as quickly as mushrooms after a rainstorm.

During the New Year's celebrations, Astana, Kazakhstan's capital city, seemed to glitter by day as well as by night. Representatives from major powers such as Russia, China, and the United States lined up to offer congratulations to President Nazarbayev and to pursue aid and cooperation agreements. Business people from the world's largest corporations were also there to look for economic deals with the country's leaders.

The year 2005 was also a landmark political year for Kazakhstan. On December 4, Nazarbayev was elected to a new seven-year term of office with 91 percent of the popular vote. In the face of persistent evidence of voting irregularities and fraud, international election observers pronounced the election results flawed but valid. Nazarbayev has been the country's leader since it achieved independence from the Soviet Union in 1991. At the

huge New Year's Eve celebration broadcast on Khabar Television, Kazakhstan's official TV station, Nazarbayev raised a glass to toast even better fortune for his country in 2006.

"I am raising this glass to you all, dear people of Kazakhstan, and to the New Year of 2006," Nazarbayev said. "May the New Year be bright for each of you."

Vast Mineral Riches

How did a sparsely populated nation in the heart of Asia, a nation that was one of the poorest in the world less than twenty years ago, achieve such overnight success?

This photograph shows the Atasu control station of the Kazakhstan-China pipeline, due to open in May 2006. Atasu, located in central Kazakhstan, will be linked to Alashenkou, in western China, by 600 miles (965 km) of pipeline transporting 210,000 barrels of Kazakh and Russian oil to China per day.

Many metals are used to make items for everyday use. Chromium is a very hard metallic element used to harden steel and other metals. Vanadium is a rare metallic element also used to harden steel and other metals. Bismuth is a metallic element used in making medicines and other metal alloys. Barite is a soft mineral mainly used in making paint. Tungsten is a metallic element used in making electric lights and in hardening steel. Molybdenum is a very hard metallic element used to harden alloys and make points for spark plugs. Phosphorite is an ore containing phosphorus, an element used in medicine, explosives, and other products. Potassium is used in making fertilizers, glass, and a number of other products. Cadmium is used in long-lasting batteries and in refining other metal alloys.

The answer, say economists, is clear: natural resources. Oil, the most important resource, has only now begun to be fully exploited. With world oil prices reaching record high levels by early 2006, billions of dollars flowed into Kazakhstan's economy.

Kazakhstan contains two-thirds of the crude oil reserves in the oil-rich Caspian Sea region. The country now exports a million **barrels** of oil a day and plans to jump to more than three million barrels a day within ten years. Experts predict that Kazakhstan will be able to pump between 1.2 billion and 1.3 billion barrels a year by 2015, making it one of the top five oil-producing nations in the world.

The single biggest development is the Tengiz oil field in the western part of Kazakhstan, which accounts for a third of the country's oil output. Tengiz is one of the top ten oil fields in the world. Much attention is now on the undeveloped Kashagan oil field in the shallow waters of the Caspian Sea. Kashagan is the world's largest find of oil since the discovery of oil in Prudhoe Bay in Alaska in 1967. In 2004, oil made up more than 57 percent of Kazakhstan's exports, and that percentage is expected to rise.

It is not just oil, however, that promises a bright future for the country. Under Kazakhstan's windswept **steppes**, deserts, and mountains also lies a treasure house of other valuable minerals. Kazakhstan has the world's largest reserves of chromium, vanadium, bismuth, barite, lead, and tungsten. It has the world's second-largest reserves of silver and zinc. In addition, the country has significant deposits of copper, gold, uranium, molybdenum, phosphorite, potassium, cadmium, and iron ore.

A Bear, a Tiger, and Uncle Sam

Like a poor person who has won the lottery, Kazakhstan's sudden economic wealth has made it a lot of new friends.

How Kazakhstan Got Its Oil

Kazakhstan's oil riches were formed long before there was a Kazakhstan or a Caspian Sea—even before there were human beings. According to the most accepted theory, hundreds of millions of years ago, the entire region of which Kazakhstan is now a part was covered by a shallow, warm sea. The Caspian Sea is today a remnant of that ancient sea. Countless rivers emptied sand and silt into the sea. As layers of sand and silt settled to the bottom, they trapped countless billions of tiny plants and animals that lived in the water. As these organisms died and decayed, they were contained in the layers. Over millions of years, the sand and silt gradually turned into rock, while the organisms, under heat and pressure, turned into the thick substance we now call crude oil. That is why oil is often categorized as "fossil fuel," since it is from the remains of fossils, or dead ancient organisms. Natural gas, also a fossil fuel, was produced in a similar way. Both oil and natural gas gather in pockets in rock formations underground.

Refining crude oil is done by temperature. Different components of crude oil boil off at different temperatures and then are condensed to make different products. The lowest temperatures produce solvents and automobile fuels, while the highest temperatures leave tar and asphalt used to build roads and make other products.

There is a joke going around Kazakhstan that when President Nazarbayev wakes up every day, he hears the growl of the Russian bear to the north and the roar of the Chinese tiger to the east. Then he opens his door to find a smiling Uncle Sam holding an empty gasoline can. The bear is the symbol of Russia, the tiger is the symbol of China, and Uncle Sam, of course, has long symbolized the United States. All three countries now see oil- and mineral-rich Kazakhstan as a vital partner and ally in Central Asia.

China, in particular, has shown great interest in Kazakhstan's oil. China now has the fastest-growing economy in the world, and many economists expect it to become the world's largest economy by 2025. In four years, China is expected to have ninety times more cars than it did only ten years ago. More than 4.5 million new cars hit the road in China in 2005 alone. With all its new cars, rapid industrial growth, and booming economy, China wants the oil it can get from nearby Kazakhstan. By May 2006, a giant oil pipeline is scheduled to open between Kazakhstan and western China. With the help of U.S. oil companies, another pipeline is being built to transport oil from the Caspian Sea region to Turkey and Russia and for shipment by sea to the United States.

A Vast Land

For much of its history, Kazakhstan has been thought of as a backwater, a remote land of great promise, but too difficult or costly to develop. Under centuries of control by Russia (from the late 1600s to 1921) and the Soviet Union (from 1921 to 1991), the country suffered greatly.

Although Kazakhstan's population today is only about 15 million people (about the same as Florida's), it is the ninth-largest country in the world in land area, covering more than 1 million square miles (2,590,000 square kilometers) (about equal to the area of the United States east of the Mississippi River). About 12 percent of the country is covered with mountains, with 44 percent desert. Much of the rest is steppe.

Ethnic Kazakhs, a people related to Turkish and **Mongol** peoples, make up half the population. The rest of the population, the result of centuries of rule by Russia, is 25 percent Russian, with smaller ethnic groups making up the rest. Slightly less than half the population (47 percent) are **Muslims**. The other major religion is the Christianity of the Russian Orthodox Church (44 percent of the population). Kazakhstan is the only nation in Central Asia that does not make Islam the official national religion.

Kazakhstan's capital city, Astana, is located on the Ishim River in one of the country's flat, semi-arid steppe regions. This 2005 photograph of the city shows modern skyscrapers, a result of the many building projects supported by profits from the oil industry.

How the Kazakhs Became One People

Today's Kazakhs are descended from a multitude of peoples who came and went across the steppes from very early times. The earliest archaeological evidence of habitation comes from 6000 B.C. when a primitive people bred cattle and horses. Those nameless tribes left primitive arrowheads and objects made of carved bone. Later peoples carved **petroglyphs** showing them to be **nomads** who wandered the steppes with their flocks and herds.

In the first century A.D. **Turkic**-speaking peoples moved into the region, followed by Mongol peoples. Both of these groups followed a nomadic way of life based on family and clan loyalties, herding, and almost constant warfare. They were superb horseback riders who learned to eat, sleep, and fight on horseback. Their diet was based on horsemeat and mare's milk. They had no written language, no cities, and no highways or river trade.

An 1820 colored engraving illustrates the dress of a Mongol shaman.

Historians believe that these early people of Kazakhstan worshipped a god that was represented by the clear blue sky. They practiced **shamanism**, which was common throughout northern Asia. The shamans, or religious leaders, would go into a trance and speak for the many spirits believed responsible for human fortunes. Forms of shamanism are still practiced today, especially in parts of Africa.

Islam and the Silk Road

In the 700s, southern Kazakhstan was influenced by a new force: Islam. The religion was brought by invading Arab armies that had conquered what is now Iraq, Iran, and Pakistan to the south. At first Islam attracted only a few people, and many years passed before it became a main religion among the nomads who wandered the Kazakh steppes.

Many Kazakhs became Muslim when the Mongol invaders converted to Islam in the late 1200s and early 1300s. Many of the Kazakh nomads,

Mongols had to be excellent archers as their clans engaged in constant warfare. A Mongol archer on horseback is illustrated in this ancient ink drawing.

Camels in a caravan loaded with goods travel along the Silk Road in ancient Kazakhstan.

however, did not convert to Islam until the 1700s and early 1800s. As a result, the roots of Islam in Kazakhstan today are not as deep as they are in neighboring Islamic countries.

In the 900s, southeastern Kazakhstan became part of the Silk Road, a system of major trade routes from China to the West. The routes became known as the Silk Road because silk was a valuable item of trade. A northern branch of the Silk Road passed near the modern Kazakhstan city of Almaty. Along it, camel caravans made their way slowly west toward the Byzantine Empire (the eastern part of the Roman Empire with its capital at Constantinople, today's Istanbul) and from there into Europe.

In trade along the Silk Road, China received grapes, cotton, chestnuts, and pomegranates from the West in exchange for Chinese silk and other products. Chinese industrial techniques such as smelting iron and making paper spread to the West along the road. Throughout the entire length of the Silk Road, culture and ideas were transmitted along with silk and other goods.

Beginning of the Kazakhs

In the early 1200s, Kazakhstan fell under the rule of one of history's great conquerors: Genghis Khan (1162–1227). Genghis Khan was a tribal leader in Mongolia who assembled a vast army of Mongol horsemen. His armies swept though much of Asia, conquering all before them. The Mongols allowed conquered peoples to practice their traditional religions.

In Kazakhstan, that was mainly shamanism, with Islam confined to cities along the Silk Road. By the time he died, Genghis Khan ruled one of the largest empires in history. It stretched from China to the edge of Europe and included all the tribes and clans of Kazakhstan.

In the years after Genghis's death, the Mongols continued to control Kazakhstan through local rulers. Gradually, the fierce Mongols intermarried and became assimilated with other Kazakh groups. One of the Turkic-speaking groups broke away from Mongol rule, calling themselves "Kazakhs," which originally meant a free person who led the life of a

Genghis Khan

Genghis Khan (*shown left*), one of history's greatest conquerors, influenced world history from China to Europe. He was born with the name Temujin in Hentiy, Mongolia, and succeeded his father as a tribal leader at age thirteen. He spent his early years uniting the tribes of Mongolia under his rule. In 1208, he changed his name to Genghis Khan ("ruler of the world"). He proceeded to lead Mongol armies to conquer northern China, then much of Central Asia. His armies marched on further, conquering many other lands, kingdoms, and empires. Genghis died in 1227, reportedly from injuries suffered after falling from his horse. At his death, the Mongol Empire stretched from the Black Sea to the Pacific Ocean. Genghis was not only a brilliant general, but also a skilled administrator. He organized his empire into divisions called khanates, some of which lasted for hundreds of years.

wanderer or adventurer. The nomads of Kazakhstan were originally called Uzbek-Kazakhs because they were members of the Uzbek tribe. They eventually dropped the term *Uzbek*. Burunduk Khan (1473–1511) was first to be called the ruler of the Kazakhs.

By the early 1500s, under the rule of Kasym Kahn, they had formed a Kazakh empire throughout much of Central Asia. It stretched from the borders of the Caspian and Aral seas to the mountains that formed the border with China. Kasym was reported to have an army of more than 200,000 horsemen, which made him feared by all his neighbors. When Kasym died central rule dissolved, and his empire split into three tribal federations, or **hordes**. These were the Elder Horde, the Middle Horde, and the Lesser Horde.

Coming of the Russians

While the hordes of Kazakhstan dealt with each other, a new power was growing to the west. The Russian Empire was rapidly expanding. In 1645, Russians set up an outpost on the north coast of the Caspian Sea. From there, they moved east and south, building more forts and seizing more territory from the three Kazakh hordes. By the 1650s, the Russians

This painting dramatizes Czar Nicholas's 1838 visit to inspect troops under Russian control in the area that was once under the control of the three hordes of Kazakhstan.

had gained full control of the region north of the Aral Sea, bringing Kazakhs into the empire as subjects of the Russian emperor, or czar.

In 1730, Abdul Kharyr of the Lesser Horde sought Russian help in a war against the Mongols. This alliance gave the Russians permanent control over the Lesser Horde. In 1798, the Russians gained control over the Middle Horde. The Elder Horde, however, managed to remain independent until the 1820s.

In the 1820s, the Russians abolished the three hordes and put all the Kazakhs into areas where they could be taxed. The Kazakhs, who had a proud tradition of independence, resisted Russian control. They revolted against the czar in 1837 and again in 1847. Both revolts were brutally suppressed, and the Russians continued to build new forts and to bring in Russians and Ukrainians to farm fertile areas of Kazakhstan.

Revolt and Repression

The Russian policy of giving Kazakh land to Russian and Ukrainian farmers continued into the twentieth century. In the six years between 1906 and 1912, for example, the Russian government established more than 500,000 farms in northern Kazakhstan. As these newcomers moved in, the Kazakhs fled eastward, toward China.

Russia's entry into World War I (1914–1918) increased the tensions between the Kazakhs and the czar's government. In 1914, the Russian government attempted to take cattle and cotton away from Kazakh farmers to help the Russian war effort. The Kazakhs resisted, and the Russians destroyed whole villages, killing all their inhabitants. In 1916, when the war against Germany and Austria-Hungary had turned badly against the Russians, they tried to recruit Kazakhs to fight in the Russian army. Many Kazakhs, who were already starving and thrown off their land, revolted. The Russians brutally crushed the revolt. Russian soldiers killed thousands of Kazakhs, while thousands more fled to China and Mongolia. Those who had taken part in the revolt and who still had land found their land taken away and given to Russian settlers.

> ## FAST FACT
>
> World War I (1914–1918) was a war primarily in Europe that pitted the Allies— Great Britain, France, Russia, and later the United States and Italy—against the Central Powers of Germany and Austria-Hungary. During the war, the Russian Revolution (1917) took place, overthrowing the czar and ending the Russian monarchy. By 1918, Germany and Austria-Hungary were defeated, and an armistice was declared. Many millions died during the war.

Soviet Rule

In 1917, when news of the Russian Revolution reached Kazakhstan, the Kazakhs revolted. They set up an independent nation, which they called Alash Orda, or the Horde of Alash. Alash Orda lasted a little over two years, from 1918 to 1920, before it was suppressed by the communists, who had taken over the government of the Russian Empire.

In 1923, the communist government in Moscow formed the **Union of Soviet Socialist Republics (USSR)**, or **Soviet Union** (1923–1989),

Russian troops march through the snow during World War I. After defeats at the hands of Germany, many Russian soldiers rebelled, setting the stage for revolution in Russia and the end of the czar's rule.

In 1917, the Russian Empire was an unhappy place. The Russian people had suffered repression for many years under the rule of the czars. They were also suffering defeat after defeat in battles with Germany during World War I. Soldiers were becoming reluctant to fight in a war merely to support the czar. A growing number of soldiers and workers actively refused to fight. This refusal led to a series of violent confrontations between the government and revolutionaries. In March, Russian troops supported the rebels in strikes and riots in Petrograd (now St. Petersburg), forcing the czar, Nicholas II, to abdicate (resign), ending more than three hundred years of rule by the **Romanov** family. The czar was replaced by a democratic government under Alexander Kerensky. Kerensky, however, refused to withdraw Russia from the war and was unable to implement economic reforms demanded by the people. In October, Kerensky's government was itself overthrown by the Bolsheviks (communists) led by Vladimir Lenin (*shown above*). Lenin's government quickly made peace with the Germans and fought a three-year civil war. All of the former Russian Empire, including Kazakhstan, was under Bolshevik rule by 1920.

a union of republics and **autonomous** regions that made up the world's biggest country in land area. The Kazakhs accepted Soviet communist rule, and a num-ber of Kazakh leaders joined the Communist Party. In 1921, Kazakhstan was officially part of the Kyrghyz Autonomous Soviet Socialist Republic (ASSR). It was not until 1936 that Kazakhstan became a full-fledged Soviet Republic, the Kazakh Soviet Socialist Republic, or Kazakh SSR.

Great Suffering

The people of Kazakhstan suffered greatly under Soviet rule, especially during the early 1930s. At that time, the Soviet Union was ruled by Joseph Stalin (1879–1953), a ruthless dictator who felt that harsh measures were nec-essary to turn the Soviet Union into a true communist state. In theory, com-munism is a system of society in which all property is owned collectively by the people. Karl Marx (1818–1883), the founder of modern communism,

Four men ride in a horse-drawn cart, working on the upper reaches of the Syr-Dar'ya in the Golodnaia Steppe region of Kazakhstan in the early 1900s. The Kazakhs' traditional, nomadic lifestyle was disrupted when Joseph Stalin was installed as leader of the Soviet Union after the Russian Revolution.

believed that only with the end of private ownership of businesses and farms would true justice and freedom come to long-suffering humanity. Marx's ideas, along with those of Vladimir Lenin (1870–1924), the leader of the Bolshevik Revolution, formed the basis of the Soviet system.

One of Stalin's main objectives was to **collectivize** farming by abolishing private ownership of farms and putting all farmers into government-run collective farms. Throughout the Soviet Union, farmers and peasants resisted collectivization. Kazakh farmers, in particular, violently objected to

Stalin's program. For them, it meant giving up a way of life thousands of years old. The Kazakhs killed their cattle and sheep rather than turn them over to the government. Thousands fled the country to China and Afghanistan. Between 1929 and 1936, it is estimated that at least 1.5 million Kazakhs fled the country and 80 percent of the livestock perished. Throughout the Soviet Union, collectivization and a famine resulting from it led to the deaths of an estimated twenty million people.

World War II

When German armies invaded the Soviet Union in 1941 during World War II (1939–1945), Stalin forcibly resettled various other peoples in Kazakhstan because he was afraid they would collaborate with the Germans. Large groups of Koreans, Germans, Ukrainians, Greeks, and others found

Joseph Stalin

The Soviet leader who had the most impact on Kazakhstan was Joseph Stalin (*shown left*). Stalin, whose real name was J.V. Dzhugashvili, was born the son of a shoemaker in Georgia, part of the Russian Empire. He joined the Communist Party as a young man and rose rapidly in its ranks as Lenin's right-hand man after the Russian Revolution. After Lenin's death in 1924, Stalin emerged from a power struggle to lead the Soviet Union. Stalin imprisoned, killed, or indirectly caused the death of millions of people within the Soviet Union. He also allowed a cult of personality to be created around himself. Such a cult emphasized not the achievements of the people as a whole, but the greatness and importance of the leader. He had villages and towns named after him. He accepted titles such as "Father of Nations" and "Gardener of Human Happiness." He also had Soviet history falsely rewritten to make it seem that he had played a more important role in establishing communism in the Russian Empire than he actually had during the revolution and afterward. Not long after Stalin's death, Soviet leaders condemned him for his brutal dictatorship and his cult of personality. Stalin's dictatorial style, however, permanently influenced other leaders who grew up in the Soviet system, including Kazakhstan's president, Nazarbayev, and Saparmurat Niyazov, the leader of Turkmenistan.

themselves in Kazakhstan. Many factories were taken apart and moved by train from western Russia to Kazakhstan to escape being captured by the Germans. The factories were then reassembled in order to continue producing for the Soviet war effort. This was a boon for the Kazakh economy and provided jobs for thousands of Kazakhs, who had been impoverished by the collectivization program in the 1930s. The Soviet Union's struggle to turn back and defeat the invading German armies in World War II is called the "Great Patriotic War" in Kazakh and Russian history books. The war ended with the complete defeat of Germany, Italy, and Japan by the Allies: Great Britain, the Soviet Union, France, and the United States.

In all, the Soviet Union is estimated to have lost more than twenty million people as a result of the war. According to today's Kazakhstan government, 1,196,164 citizens of Kazakhstan served in the Soviet army during World War II. More than 400,000 of them were killed or wounded fighting for the Soviet Union.

Kazakhstan after the War

In the late 1950s and early 1960s, Soviet leaders tried to turn vast areas of northern Kazakhstan into fertile farmlands under the Virgin and Idle

 The Cold War

Right after World War II, Kazakhstan, as part of the Soviet Union, found itself in a worldwide struggle called the Cold War (1945–1990). The Cold War was a battle for political, economic, and cultural dominance of the world between a group of communist nations, led by the Soviet Union, and a group of Western nations, led by the United States. It is called the Cold War because it never developed into a "hot war" between the United States and the Soviet Union. Nevertheless, the two nations engaged in a nuclear arms race and sponsored small, nonnuclear conflicts around the world. On two occasions, the Korean War (1950–1953) and the Vietnam War (1964–1975), the Cold War turned into armed conflict between communist and noncommunist nations, but not directly between the United States and the Soviet Union. They also competed to see who would lead the world in the conquest of space. That competition was known as the space race. The Cold War even spread to sports. In 1980, U.S. president Jimmy Carter ordered a U.S. boycott of the Olympic Games in Moscow to protest the Soviet invasion of Afghanistan in 1979.

Lands Program. Land that had never before been farmed came under the plow. As a result of all the new farms, Kazakhstan emerged as the Soviet Union's major wheat producer, and wheat remains today a major farm crop in Kazakhstan. The new farmlands also brought another rush of about two million Russian and Ukrainian farmers into Kazakhstan by the late 1960s. In the 1970s and 1980s, Soviet leader Leonid Brezhnev, concerned that the birthrate among Kazakhs was higher than among ethnic Russians, encouraged Russians to settle in Kazakhstan by giving them land and money for resettlement and for producing more children. Today, ethnic Russians make up 30 percent of Kazakhstan's population. Ethnic Kazakhs make up a bare majority—53 percent—of Kazakhstan's population.

The Soviet Union also began using Kazakhstan's vast empty spaces to test nuclear weapons in its struggle with the United States as part of the Cold War. From 1949 to 1989, the Soviet Union conducted about 460 nuclear weapons tests at Semipalatinsk, including explosions on the ground, in the atmosphere, and underground. Five of the tests were not successful and released radioactive plutonium into the environment. Starting in 1961, more than 300 test explosions were conducted underground at the

The era of nuclear testing by the Soviet Union in Kazakhstan came to an end when, in a cooperative effort, an explosion set off by U.S. and Kazakh scientists sealed off the last remaining tunnel of a testing facility in Semipalatinsk in 2000.

site. According to the **International Atomic Energy Agency (IAEA)**, a **United Nations (UN)** agency, thirteen of the underground tests released radioactive gases into the atmosphere. The IAEA, however, has found no lasting radioactive contamination resulting from the tests.

Kazakhstan also became the main staging ground for the Soviet Union's space program. The Baikonur Cosmodrome in western Kazakhstan was built in 1955 as a long-range missile test site and later expanded to include space flights. Many famous space flights originated at Baikonur, including the launching of the first artificial space satellite (Sputnik 1 on October 4, 1957) and the first manned orbital flight (by Yuri Gagarin in 1961). Today, the Russians lease the Cosmodrome from the Kazakhstan government for $115 million per year and Russian rockets still regularly blast into space from Kazakhstan soil.

The Soviet Union Falls Apart

By 1990, political and economic troubles were building up within Kazakhstan and the whole Soviet Union. Loud voices called for the breakup of the rule of the Communist Party and for more power to the individual republics. The loudest of all was Boris Yeltsin, who was elected head of the **Russian Soviet Federated Socialist Republic (RSFSR)**. The RSFSR was by far the largest and most powerful Soviet republic and generally was able to dictate to the other republics of the Soviet Union. Yeltsin, as head of the RSFSR, was the most powerful man in

FAST FACT

The collapse of the Soviet Union produced fifteen new countries: the Baltic nations of Estonia, Lithuania, and Latvia; the Eastern European nations of Russia, Ukraine, Belarus, and Moldova; the Central Asian nations of Kazakhstan, Kyrgyzstan, Tajikistan, Uzbekistan, and Turkmenistan; and the Caucasus Mountains nations of Georgia, Armenia, and Azerbaijan.

the Soviet Union at the time. On June 12, 1990, the legislature of the RSFSR, led by Yeltsin, voted to declare itself independent of the Soviet Union. In July, Yeltsin quit the Communist Party.

The loss of the RSFSR was a death-blow for the Soviet Union. On August 18, 1991, a group of dedicated communists led a coup against Mikhail Gorbachev, the leader of the Soviet Union, hoping to gain control of the RSFSR and hold the other Soviet republics in line. Gorbachev was held under house arrest in the Crimea, the area of southern Russia where he was vacationing. Yeltsin rushed to the White House of Russia, the building housing his RSFSR presidential offices in Moscow, to defy the coup. Soldiers supporting the coup defected to Yeltsin and Gorbachev was rescued and returned to Moscow. The Soviet Union, however, was finished. In November 1991, Yeltsin issued a decree banning the Communist Party throughout the RSFSR. Soon after, the other parts of the Soviet Union followed the RSFSR's lead.

Kazakhstan Declares Independence

One by one, the republics that made up the Soviet Union followed Yeltsin's lead and declared independence. Kazakhstan declared itself independent on December 16, 1991. On December 25, Gorbachev resigned as president of the Soviet Union. By December 31, all official Soviet government institutions had stopped operating. The Soviet flag was lowered for the last time over the Kremlin, the once-feared center of Soviet power.

In Kazakhstan, independence was greeted with great joy. Still, independence brought its own worries and problems. The most immediate problem facing Nazarbayev, the president of the new nation, was the 1,140 nuclear weapons that the Soviets had left behind in Kazakhstan. Instead of keeping the weapons and making Kazakhstan an instant nuclear power, Nazarbayev decided to dismantle them. He asked U.S. experts to come into the country to help destroy them.

Another immediate problem facing Kazakhstan was its economy. During its years as part of the Soviet Union, the country's economy was heavily dependent on Russia's economy. Immediately after independence, the Kazakh economy plunged into depression, shrinking by 50 percent between 1991 and 1994 alone. Slowly, however, the economy began to improve and then, by 1999, to expand, led by increases in world oil prices. Today, the Kazakh economy is one of the fastest growing economies in the world.

The Kazakh New Year was celebrated in Independence Square on March 22, 2004, with a time-honored ceremony featuring women in traditional dress.

On the Road to Democracy?

Democracy, as Americans know it, has never been a tradition in Kazakhstan. In the past, the country has been ruled by tribal leaders, khans, kings, czars, and communist dictators. All the country's past governments have had elements of democracy, but real authority has always been in the hands of a few leaders or party officials.

Members of the Kazakh election commission empty a ballot box to count votes in the December 2005 presidential election. Nursultan Nazarbayev won a second seven-year term in a controversial result.

When independence came in 1991, Kazakhstan retained the basic government structure it had before. It also kept most of the same leaders who were in power under the Soviets, from Nazarbayev on down.

In 1995, Kazakhstan adopted a new, post-Soviet constitution that gave the country a government structure that bears similarity to that of the United States. Kazakhstan has a president elected by popular vote to a seven-year term. It has a seventy-seven-member assembly (similar to the U.S. House of Representatives), most of whom are directly elected; a forty-seven-member senate, forty of whose members are chosen by the leaders of Kazakhstan's fourteen regions (similar to U.S. states) and seven appointed by the president. It also has a judiciary, or national court system, to complete the three branches of its government.

Zharmakhan Tuyakbai (shown above), *President Nazarbayev's challenger in the 2005 election, has spoken out against the president, saying "Every year he strengthens his own, limitless power. Mr. Nazarbayev is moving toward the status of dictator."*

Rigged Election?

While the government structure of Kazakhstan seems democratic, critics say that the country is anything but a democracy. They charge that the political system has become increasingly **authoritarian** and that President Nazarbayev shows signs of developing his own personality cult.

To many, Nazarbayev's margin of victory in the December 2005 election was simply too good to be true. He won the election by getting a startling 91 percent of the vote. Nazarbayev's closest challenger, Zharmakhan Tuyakbai, won 6.6 percent of the vote. Seventy-seven percent of all registered voters had cast ballots. Tuyakbai and others accused Nazarbayev supporters of intimidating voters and rigging the election results. "The sheer scale of the victory has surprised even the most seasoned analysts," reported *Asia Pulse*, a news service that covers Asian events.

Sergei Duvanov, a prominent Kazakh opposition journalist, and three other activists were arrested a week after the election. They had chained themselves to stone partitions in the main square of Kazakhstan's capital city, Astana, to protest the election. They held up signs that read "91 percent of national shame" and "91 percent back to the Soviet Union." "We are protesting the unfair election," Duvanov said. "We want to show that not everyone is a coward in this country."

The opposition parties protested that they were denied any significant access to the media to get their message across to the voters. It is actually against the law in Kazakhstan to criticize the president.

Kazakh journalist Sergei Duvanov was arrested for publicly protesting the 2005 election results. He had been arrested and imprisoned before on false charges after he published an article linking President Nazarbayev to illegal bank accounts.

Outside Observers

About 1,600 observers monitored the 2005 presidential elections, including some 465 from the **Organization for Security and Cooperation in Europe (OSCE)**. "I much regret that the Kazakh authorities did not provide a level playing field for democratic elections. This happened despite assurances from the president that the elections would be free and fair," said Audrey Glover, head of the OSCE's observer mission in Kazakhstan.

Much of the OSCE's criticism focused on the election campaign, saying that the opposition was denied equal coverage in state media and that its supporters faced intimidation, beatings, and seizure of campaign materials. For example, the OSCE said that there was evidence of university students being pressured by faculty members to vote for Nazarbayev. The OSCE reported incidents of ballot stuffing (people voting more than one time) and pressure on voters. Counting procedures were violated and election results were skewed.

The OSCE monitors, however, praised the country for holding an election that was open to opposition candidates. Compared to Kazakhstan's past and compared to the other ex-Soviet nations of Central Asia, Kazakhstan is the most democratic. Most Kazakhs, even Nazarbayev's strongest critics, say that he most likely would have won the election even if it had been completely open and fair, although not by such a huge margin. The president is popular because economic prosperity and stability have come to Kazakhstan. While corruption is said to be widespread, life is definitely getting better for many people.

On the streets of Almaty, Kazakhstan's largest city, most people interviewed just before the election by the British Broadcasting Corporation (BBC) thought their country was on the right track. "Of course I'll go and vote," said one woman. "I'll vote for the president, Nursultan Nazarbayev, naturally." Another voter said, "We should choose stability, and [Nazarbayev] is not the worst there is."

International observers have also criticized other elections in Kazakhstan as neither free nor fair. Parliamentary elections last year were widely seen as rigged.

Freedom of the Press

Freedom of the **press** is generally considered to be essential to ensuring true democracy. In modern democratic nations, such as the United States and Great Britain, freedom of the press is considered a key check on abuse of governmental power, since reporters are free to call attention to corruption, fraud, abuse, incompetence, and misuse of power at all levels of government. In the United States, this freedom is enshrined in the First Amendment to the Constitution. In part, the amendment states, "Congress shall make no law ... abridging the freedom of speech, or of the press." If there were not a First Amendment, a law could be passed, for example, saying that anyone who criticizes the president could be punished by being thrown into jail. Kazakhstan's law making it a crime to "insult" the president can be considered such a law, since what might be called an insult is open to interpretation.

Family Business and Freedom of the Press

A major criticism against Nazarbayev is that he has promoted members of his family to important positions. His wife, daughters, sister-in-law, and son-in-law all hold important positions. While this practice is not unusual in traditional Kazakh society, where family and clan relations have been important for centuries, critics say it does not promote democracy. Nazarbayev's sister-in-law, Svetlana, for example, is accused of using her role as the head of the printing press used by opposition newspapers to block articles critical of the president.

Nazarbayev's eldest daughter, Dariga, is an opera singer who holds a doctorate in political science and, along with her husband, heads a media empire that includes radio, television, and newspapers. Another daughter, Dinara, controls a bank. A third daughter, Aliya, is a developer of luxury property. Many outsiders believe that Dariga is being groomed to succeed her father as Kazakhstan's president.

Nazarbayev has said that he supports freedom of the press for Kazakhstan, but many critics privately dispute that. While freedom of the press is written into Kazakhstan's 1995 constitution, outside observers say that

Opposition bloc candidate Zharmakhan Tuyakbai speaks to reporters outside a polling station during the 2005 presidential election. Tuyakbai was once a strong figure in the president's own Otan party, but quit his post as Speaker in parliament in protest over what he felt were rigged elections.

Dariga Nazarbayeva

Besides President Nazarbayev himself, the president's eldest daughter, Dariga Nazarbayeva (*shown left*), may be the most watched official in Kazakhstan. Nazarbayeva is an acclaimed opera singer who also holds a doctoral degree in political science. Many believe that she is being groomed to succeed her father as Kazakhstan's president. Nazarbayeva has founded a new political party called Asar (Kazakh for "together"), which she says was founded with her father's "permission." Asar so far has 230,000 members, second only to her father's Otan party.

Nazarbayeva makes no secret that she is thinking of one day becoming Kazakhstan's president, although she will not say that she actually wants the job. Critics say that Asar is designed to make her into a serious politician with a large following, particularly among young people, so she can run for president in 2012. They worry that the presidency might be handed down from father to daughter more like a kingdom than a democracy.

A few years ago, Nazarbayeva dismissed that charge. "We are not a monarchy," she told a reporter. "We prefer that [the succession to the presidency] will happen [naturally] as in the Bush family."

media not friendly to the government have been harassed and censored. In 2004, the International Federation of Journalists identified a "growing pattern" of intimidation of the media in Kazakhstan. "Insulting" the president or other officials is officially a crime. The private life, health, and financial affairs of the president are classified as an "official state secret" so they are never reported in the media or known to the general public.

Journalists who violate these rules are not usually arrested, but they are often "taught a lesson," according to *Global Journalist* magazine. For example, in 2002, *Global Journalist* reported that Sergei Duvanov, the antigovernment journalist arrested after the 2005 election, was assaulted outside his apartment by three masked men. "You know why we're doing this," they said as they beat him. "Next time we'll make you a cripple." Duvanov was hospitalized with a concussion. According to Human Rights Watch, "coming on the heels of Duvanov's courageous reporting and in light of the Kazakh government's general intolerance of independent media, it is difficult to dismiss this attack as a simple act of [violence]." *Global Journalist* describes other incidents and other ways it says the Kazakh government suppresses independent press reporting in Kazakhstan without actually banning publications.

U.S. Encouragement

The United States is a strong ally of Kazakhstan and President Nazarbayev. On October 13, 2005, not long before Nazarbayev was reelected, U.S. secretary of state Condoleezza Rice visited Kazakhstan. She praised President Nazarbayev for

U.S. secretary of state Condoleezza Rice (far left) *visited with Kazakh president Nursultan Nazarbayev* (far right) *in October 2005 to discuss U.S. investment in Kazakhstan. They were joined by Kazakhstan's ambassador to the United States, Kanat Saudabayev* (second from left), *and foreign minister, Kosymzhomart Tokayev.*

leading in the fight against terrorism and for his support of "international security." Secretary Rice also said, "Kazakhstan has an unprecedented opportunity to lead Central Asia toward a future of democracy and elevate U.S.-Kazakhstan relations to a new level.... Kazakhstan's greatest days lie ahead of it. And the United States wants to be your partner."

After the election, the United States said that Kazakhstan should investigate charges of fraud in its presidential election and repair any shortcomings in the electoral process. Matthew J. Bryza, deputy assistant secretary of state for European and Eurasian affairs, described the vote as "a step forward but not as far as we had hoped."

"Not Ready for Democracy"

President Nazarbayev has promised to investigate alleged fraud in the recent elections, but he also insists that his country is moving slowly and surely toward a more democratic future. He has said that the Kazakhs, after centuries of autocratic rule, are not ready for full democracy. "Democracy is a culture which society has to learn over time," he said in a November 2005 speech.

In an interview with the *Washington Times* newspaper, the Kazakh leader again warned that Americans should not expect his country to become fully democratic overnight. "One must understand the process of building a democracy in Kazakhstan," Nazarbayev said. Not long ago, "the Soviet Union was in power here, and for a long period Kazakhstan was part of this system. It is very hard for us to learn democratic values all at once."

Nazarbayev also stressed the role that the United States and U.S. businesses could play in building a strong, stable, and democratic Kazakhstan. "We are learning from American democracy—even in resolving ethnic tension—and American investment is creating jobs. The American way of doing business is very attractive.... Today we have 300 American companies working in Kazakhstan, among them the huge corporations of Mobil, Texaco, Amoco, and Chevron. We have attracted $3 billion from the U.S. with our huge supply of... oil and gas."

On January 30, 2005, President Nazarbayev met with the leader of the Ak Zhol opposition party, Alikhan Baymenov, to spur political reform. Earlier that year, the Kazakh head of state expressed the need to set up a state commission to work out a program of further political reforms.

CHAPTER 5

The Other "Stans"

When the Soviet Union dissolved in 1991, Central Asia was left with four other new independent countries besides Kazakhstan: Kyrgyzstan (KEER-gez-stahn), Tajikistan (tah-JEEK-e-stahn), Turkmenistan (turk-MEN-e-stahn), and Uzbekistan

The five "Stans" of the former Soviet Republic cover almost 1,544,000 square miles (4 million square kilometers), more than 40 percent of the area of the United States. Their topography varies widely, with Tajikistan and Kyrgyzstan containing mountains and river valleys compared to Kazakhstan and Turkmenistan's flat deserts. Uzbekistan is bordered by the four other "Stans." Its heavily irrigated river valleys are necessary due to its landlocked position. All five "Stans" are rich in natural resources, but only Kazakhstan has been able to exploit theirs to jumpstart an economy that is now thriving.

(ooz-BEK-e-stahn). Today, while Kazakhstan has a thriving economy, the other four "stans" are not doing as well.

Kyrgyzstan

When Kyrgyzstan became independent of the Soviet Union in 1991, there were high hopes that it would survive as a democracy. Those hopes, however, were soon dashed as corruption and repression under President Askar Akayev grew. The president reportedly began enriching himself and his family while living standards in the small mountainous republic declined. Outside observers found that elections under Akayev were rigged and that opposition figures regularly faced beatings and imprisonment.

While Kyrgyzstan does have some oil and gas resources, they are undeveloped, and the country must import much of what it needs.

Kyrgyzstan is also one of the poorest of the five Central Asian republics, with a poverty rate (percentage of the population living below an officially set poverty level) at more than 40 percent. Most of the country's wealthy people live in the north, near the capital of Bishkek, while the southern part of the country is desperately poor.

Throughout much of the 1990s, corruption scandals, a failing economy, and growing political unrest plagued Akayev's government. In two rounds of parliamentary elections on February 27 and March 13, 2005, popular unrest boiled over. Charges of voter fraud by the ruling party grew, starting in the southern part of the country. On March 14, fifteen thousand people marched and called for the resignation of Akayev. The rioters seized the main government building in Bishkek. Akayev fled to Kazakhstan, then to Moscow. He officially resigned his office on April 4.

A poster of former Kyrgyzstan president Askar Akayev burns in Osh, Kyrgyzstan, in March 2005 during a rally of opposition activists. President Akayev resigned later in the year under pressure from a corruption scandal.

In July 2005, Kurmanbek Bakiev was elected Kyrgyzstan's new president by a landslide 88.9 percent of the popular vote. Bakiev campaigned on a promise to end corruption and fight poverty. In October, Bakiev reached an agreement with the United States to allow U.S. forces to continue to use the Manas military base near Bishkek for operations in Afghanistan. More than seventeen hundred U.S. troops and millions of gallons of fuel pass through the base every month. In the past, the United States paid about $50 million a year to use the base, but Bakiev believes that some of the money was stolen by the son of ousted president Akayev.

Tajikistan

Tajikistan is the smallest nation in Central Asia in land area. It is landlocked (having no sea coast) and almost entirely covered by the Pamir mountain range, with more than 50 percent of the country 10,000 feet (3,050 meters) above sea level.

Almost immediately after becoming independent in 1991, Tajikistan was thrown into a violent civil war between supporters of the Moscow-backed government of President Emomali Rahmonov and supporters of an opposition group who wanted a government based on the principles of Islam. The war ended in 1997 with a peace

agreement arranged by the UN, but up to fifty thousand people were killed in the fighting and more than one-tenth of Tajikistan's six million people had fled the country. Peaceful elections were held in 1999, reelecting Rahmonov, but the opposition declared them unfair.

The country is still struggling with economic and social problems stemming from the years of fighting, despite good growth in its economy after the end of the war. In 2001, Tajikistan was hit by drought and famine, and it still requires interna-

A Russian helicopter carrying supplies to troops stationed along the Tajik-Afghan border is guided by a smoke flare to the landing pad on one of the many peaks in the mountainous region. A Russian soldier in the foreground watches the aircraft land.

tional aid today for a significant part of the population. Some money comes from the increasing trade in drugs, mainly opium, from neighboring Afghanistan. Tajikistan is the first stop on the illegal drug route from Afghanistan to Russia and Europe. Tajikistan remains, however, the poorest country in Central Asia.

Russia still plays a strong role in Tajikistan. In October 2004, the Russians opened a military base in the capital city of Dushnabe. Russian troops also guarded sections of the border between Tajikistan and Afghanistan until the summer of 2005.

Turkmenistan

Turkmenistan is made up mainly of desert and, as of 2005, has the smallest population (4,952,081) of the five former Soviet Central Asian republics. Despite having the world's fifth-largest reserves of natural gas and large amounts of oil, Turkmenistan still suffers from widespread poverty. Unlike neighboring Kazakhstan, Turkmenistan has been unable to attract foreign investment to develop its resources.

Turkmenistan is considered one of the most repressive and dictatorial countries in the world. Today, only one political party is allowed there—President Saparmurat Niyazov's Democratic Party of Turkmenistan, which is made up of former members

A statue of Turkmen president Saparmurat Niyazov in Ashgabat, Turkmenistan, is guarded by soldiers. Niyazov keeps control of the country by eliminating financial support for the education system and health care and restricting the flow of information in and out of Turkmenistan.

of the Communist Party. In Niyazov's Turkmenistan, there is no independent radio, TV, or newspaper to counter the ones controlled by the government. Government officials monitor all media outlets, operate the printing presses, and lay down guidelines as to what the people can read, see, and hear. In 2002, OSCE said that the lack of press freedom in Turkmenistan was "unprecedented" in OSCE history.

In November 2002, gunmen fired on a car carrying President Niyazov. Niyazov was unhurt, but he blamed the attack on an opposition group. Others accused him of staging the attack in order to shut down all political opposition. Within weeks, the opposition leader, Boris Shikhmuradov, was arrested and sentenced to life imprisonment. Niyazov then declared himself president for life.

Niyazov calls himself Turkmenbashi, or "Father of the Turkmen." Turkmen are supposed to take spiritual guidance from his book *Ruhnama (Book of the Soul)*, a collection of his thoughts. Adults are supposed to read it every Saturday. In 2005, the book was blasted into space on a Russian rocket "to conquer space," said an article in the official Turkmenistani newspaper. Niyazov has, according to strict Muslim laws, banned young men from wearing beards and long hair and forbidden the playing of recorded music on television and at weddings.

In 2004, Niyazov ordered the construction of a palace made of ice in the heart of the Turkmenistani desert. "Our children can learn to ski. We can build cafes there, and restaurants," he said in a televised speech. In 2005, Niyazov ordered the closing of all

hospitals in the country except those in Ashgabat, the capital. He is reported to have said, "Why do we need such hospitals? If people are ill, they can come to Ashgabat."

Uzbekistan

Ancient Uzbekistan was at the heart of the Silk Road trade with majestic cities and centers of culture such as Bukhara and Samarkand. Today, fifteen years after leaving the Soviet Union, Uzbekistan, with almost twenty-seven million people, is the most populous of the former Central Asian republics.

It has been a rocky road, however, for the former Soviet republic. The country has remained a tightly controlled dictatorship in which no freedom of the press and no political opposition to the government are allowed. President Islam Karimov, who, like Nazarbayev in Kazakhstan, was Communist Party chief before independence, has allowed little freedom.

A 2004 UN report condemned Uzbekistan's record on human rights and described "systematic" use of torture by the government against suspected political opponents. In April 2004, the European Bank for Reconstruction and Development announced that it was slashing aid to Uzbekistan because of the government's failure to reform and its poor record on human rights.

Unlike in Kazakhstan, Uzbekistan's government has not reformed its economic system to allow foreign investors to develop the country and to encourage businesses to grow. Just as when it was a Soviet communist republic, most economic decisions are made by the government as part of centralized planning. In recent years, the economy has been stagnant. A World Bank report in the summer of 2003 found Uzbekistan's living standards and economic growth among the lowest of all the now independent nations that once made up the Soviet Union.

Political unrest has also plagued Uzbekistan. In May 2005, government troops fired on protesters in the eastern city of Andijan. The protesters had gathered to protest the jailing of people charged with "Islamic **extremism**." Although a Muslim himself, Karimov fears that Islamic terrorists want to overthrow his government and replace it with a state run according to **sharia**, Islamic law based on the Koran, the Muslim holy book. Witnesses reported a bloodbath at Andijan, with several hundred civilian deaths. The government says that 180 people died.

Shortly after the terrorist attacks on the United States on September 11, 2001, Uzbekistan allowed the United States to use an air base at Karshi-Kanabad to support U.S. operations in Afghanistan. When the United States joined the European Union in calling for an independent investigation of the protest at Andijan, relations cooled. President Karimov moved closer to Russia and China, who refused to criticize Uzbekistan's leaders. In July 2005, the government of Uzbekistan ordered the United States to leave the Karshi-Kanabad air base.

A billboard picturing Uzbekistan's president, Islam Karimov, stands in the religiously conservative Fergana Valley in the town of Andijan, east of Tashkent. The words on the poster urge the region's residents to protect the nation's borders from Islamic extremists.

CHAPTER 6

Golden Future?

In a speech in Kazakhstan on October 13, 2005, U.S. secretary of state Condoleezza Rice said that the United States hopes that Kazakhstan will lead the other countries of Central Asia away from dictatorship toward democracy. She urged Kazakhstan and the other countries of the region to shake off "the old devils of extremism and authoritarianism" and "unleash the creative energy of their people to secure a future of freedom, prosperity, and stability."

President Nazarbayev promised that his country is now ready for further democratic reforms, if not for full democracy on the Western model. He also predicted even more spectacular economic progress ahead. In his inauguration speech on January 11, the Kazakh president predicted another "golden year" for Kazakhstan. He pledged to use his new seven-year term as president to double salaries and pensions. "In seven years [Kazakhstan's] economy will double and we will be on the level of Eastern European countries," Nazarbayev said.

A Kazakh woman visits a monument in Astana called the Baiterek, which is decorated with President Nazarbayev's right handprint. When the visitor places her palm on the handprint, the national anthem of Kazakhstan plays from a speaker in the monument.

The "Iron Silk Road"

One of the great projects that Nazarbayev is counting on is what some are now calling the "Iron Silk Road"—a rail link through Kazakhstan, Turkmenistan, Iran, and Turkey that will connect China with Europe. Goods and passengers would be able to travel on the Iron Silk Road from China to Europe in as few as eight days. Today, most trade between China and Europe goes by sea, taking forty to fifty days. A portion also goes along the Trans-Siberian railroad, a rail line that crosses Russia's vast northern wilderness of Siberia. Transport along the Trans-Siberian takes fifteen days. Kazakh and Chinese leaders believe that all along the route of the new railway, local economies will blossom, new towns will spring up, and jobs will be created. Just as in the past, when the Silk Road turned parts of Central Asia into centers of culture and civilization, supporters of the Iron Silk Road hope that Central Asia will once again blossom.

The project, however, which is expected to be completed in 2010 at a cost of $6.7 billion, requires the cooperation of a number of governments. The easiest part of the project will be passage through Kazakhstan. "Building here is easy; you won't see a mountain for hundreds of [miles]," says Kanat Zhangaskin, vice president of Kazakhstan's national railway company. "It makes perfect sense to reopen this ancient trade route."

Chinese president Hu Jintao is a big supporter of the new rail link, and Chinese companies have pledged billions of dollars to help build it. China is also spending $750 million to improve and modernize its own railroad links to the Kazakhstan border. Along with the new railroad, Chinese and Kazakh leaders also hope to build modern highway systems and **telecommunications** links, eventually producing a vast, efficient transportation and communication system through Central Asia.

The United States is also supporting the project, as it will enable the United States to get oil and other goods more cheaply than transporting them by sea. "We are building a new Silk Road, but the commodities now are not silk and spices, they are oil and gas. The paths will be taken not by camels and caravans, but by pipelines, fiber optics, and railroads," said former U.S. energy secretary Frederico Pena.

New Pipelines

Companies are also improving old oil pipelines and building new pipelines that should allow Kazakhstan to increase its oil output to three million barrels per day. A pipeline between

Kazakhstan's Tengiz oil field and the Russian port of Novorossiysk was opened in 2001 and is now being improved by a group of oil companies. A new oil pipeline carrying oil from Kazakhstan's two giant Caspian Sea oil fields to western China is scheduled to open in May 2006. China's booming economy is starved for oil, and Kazakhstan is a close and safe source.

Space Power?

Kazakhstan may soon become the world's newest power in the space business. Within seven years, Kazakhstan is planning to launch six satellites, plus two satellites launched jointly with Russia, from the Baikonur Cosmodrome. The satellites will make it possible to forecast earthquakes, monitor the level of radiation, study natural resources, and, above all, bring telephone, TV, and Internet connections to every remote settlement in the country.

Space exploration and development make money for Kazakhstan from other countries besides Russia, including the United States. The Baikonur Cosmodrome can put a satellite into orbit for any country at a lower cost than that charged by the U.S. National Aeronautics and Space Administration (NASA). The launch site used to be guarded with secrecy,

A Russian rocket is mounted to the launch pad at the Baikonur Cosmodrome in April 2004. The flag of the United States, one of the countries that utilizes the facility, can be seen flying in the upper left corner of the photograph. Thanks to the booming economy, Kazakhstan hopes to launch a rocket of its own into space in the near future.

but it has been open to the public since 1991 under certain conditions.

Water Problems

While oil is flowing out of Kazakhstan's underground reservoirs and money is flowing into government treasuries, the flow of another vital element—water—could present problems for the country in the future. Most of Kazakhstan's farms are irrigated by river water. Many of the rivers that supply the irrigation canals are fed by glaciers and permafrost in the Tian Shan mountains. The glaciers, however, are melting fast—so fast, say scientists, that the livelihood of millions of Kazakhs and Chinese on the other side of the border could be affected.

The UN has warned that Lake Balkhash, the second largest lake in Central Asia, could actually dry up, creating an environmental crisis in Kazakhstan. There is less and less water coming into the lake, which has already shrunk by 770 square miles (1,994 sq km). Lake Balkhash gets most of its water from the Ili River, which

flows into Kazakhstan from western China. The main worry of Kazakh leaders concerns China's plan to divert most of the river to support the rapid development of western China.

Kazakhstan fears that the same thing could happen to Lake Balkhash that happened to the Aral Sea, Central Asia's largest lake, in western Kazakhstan. The Aral Sea has turned into two separate water reservoirs surrounded by vast wastelands, a result of Soviet policy to divert its two feeder rivers for cotton irrigation. So much water was extracted that the lake began to dry up, causing widespread devastation along its banks.

To make matters worse, Lake Balkhash is already intensively polluted

Kazakhstan's water problem is illustrated in this picture of the Aral Sea, taken near the settlement of Dzhambul. In 1987, the world's fourth-largest salt lake dried up enough to split into two parts. Camels pass between the two new, smaller lakes on land that is now a graveyard home to rusty shipwrecks.

by industrial waste and sewage. Half of Kazakhstan's population uses water that is not up to international standards of cleanliness. According to the United Nations, Kazakhstan has the least quantity of clean drinking water available per person in the whole of the former Soviet Union.

City of Dreams

Much of President Nazarbayev's vision of the future for Kazakhstan revolves around Astana, the capital city he rebuilt beginning in 1997. Once an obscure fortress town of the Russian Empire, Astana today is a fast-growing metropolis of 600,000 residents. The Kazakh government is spending billions of dollars to construct government buildings, museums, monuments, religious shrines, entertainment places, apartment buildings, and hospitals.

Everyone in Kazakhstan knows how dear to Nazarbayev's heart the new capital is. "The heart of the nation now beats here," he proudly informed his people in 1999, two years after officially uprooting the government from Almaty, the former capital. Nazarbayev is said to be the planner behind Astana's every detail, right down to the choice of yellow and white paints for the houses.

Nazarbayev has employed world-famous architects, such as Lord Norman Foster from London, to design buildings that are unique in the world. Foster is the designer of what is being called the "Palace of Peace." This structure, due to open in August 2006, was inspired by two wonders of the ancient world: the Great Pyramid of Egypt and the Hanging Gardens of Babylon. The pyramid-shaped building will dominate the skyline of Astana. At the building's bottom will be a sunken opera house. A museum of culture and a "university of civilization" will take up the pyramid's lower floors. Zigzag ramps will lead visitors upward through clusters of tropical plants, guided by light from blue-and-gold stained glass at the top of the pyramid. At the very top, Nazarbayev wants a circular chamber suspended in air by four huge support beams that "symbolize the hands of peace." Nazarbayev hopes that two hundred delegates from the world's main religions will meet in the chamber every four years to promote world peace. A research center of the world's religions, complete with a large library, will occupy the floor below.

From his large palace, Nazarbayev can survey his entire city. Each distinctive building has been given a nickname by locals: An oddly shaped ministry is known as the "cigarette lighter," a bright yellow group of apartments is called the "banana," and a spaceship-shaped building housing a circus and lions is nicknamed "the UFO."

The Baiterek ("Tree of Life" in Kazakh) is Astana's highest monument. It is supposed to depict a soaring sheaf of wheat, on top of which lies the golden egg of a roc, a mythical bird of Arabic and Central Asian legend so large and strong it supposedly could carry off large animals. (Out of range of the president's ears, many Kazakhs call the Baiterek "the lollipop.") The Baiterek is composed of a trunk of white metal that weighs 1,000 tons (907 metric tons) and shoots up 344 feet (105 m) from the ground, separating into branches holding a golden glass ball that is 72 feet (22 m) in diameter and weighs 300 tons (272 metric tons). Visitors can take an elevator to the top of the monument and into the ball, which gives a 360-degree view of the city. The main attraction inside the ball is a silver mold of Nazarbayev's own palm print. Placing a hand in it strikes up the Kazakh national anthem. At night, the monument is lit by pulsating purple and turquoise lights.

Kazakhstan's new capital city symbolizes its glittering future. As its economy continues to grow and its citizens prosper, the future looks to be one of progress and growth.

The Palace of Peace, a monument being built as a national center for Kazakhstan's various ethnic and geographical groups, was designed by British architect Norman Foster. The form of a pyramid—measuring 203 feet (62 meters) high with a 203-by-203-foot (62-by-62-m) base—represents diversity unified. The structure will be clad in stone with glazed windows telling people what activities and functions are taking place inside. The apex will be decorated with stained glass designed by artist Brian Clarke.

Time Line

1st–8th centuries	Turkic-speaking and Mongol tribes invade and settle in what is now Kazakhstan.
700s	Arab invaders introduce Islam.
1219–1224	Mongols under Genghis Khan invade.
1400s	The Kazakhs emerge as a distinct group.
1500s	The Kazakhs split into three tribal groups that are led by khans.
1731–1820s	Russia gains control of the lands of the three hordes.
1822–1868	Russia dissolves the hordes and divides Kazakh.
1868–1916	Thousands of Russian and Ukrainian peasants settle Kazakh lands; the first industries are set up.
1917	Civil war breaks out following the communist revolution in Russia.
1920s–1930s	Widespread famine affects Kazakhstan.
1923	Kazakhstan becomes a self-governing republic of the Soviet Union.
1936	Kazakhstan becomes a full union republic of the Soviet Union.
1949	The first Soviet nuclear test explosion is carried out in eastern Kazakhstan.
1960s	About two million people, mainly Russians, move to Kazakhstan during the campaign to develop virgin lands.
1961	The first manned spacecraft is launched from the Baikonur space launch site in central Kazakhstan.
1991	The Soviet Union is dissolved; Kazakhstan becomes an independent country.
1995	Kazakhstan adopts a new constitution expanding the president's powers.
1997	President Nazarbayev moves Kazakhstan's capital from Almaty to Astana.
1999	Nazarbayev is reelected for another term as Kazakh president.
2001	In March, the first major pipeline for transporting oil from the Caspian Sea to world markets opens.
2004	Construction begins on an oil pipeline to the Chinese border.
2005	Nazarbayev is elected to another seven-year term.
2006	The Kazakhstan-China oil pipeline is due to be completed in May.

Glossary

authoritarian requiring unquestioning obedience to an authority, usually a political leader

autonomous self-governing in internal matters

barrels units of measure for crude oil equaling 31 gallons (117 liters)

collectivize to establish group ownership of property

ethnic describing a group with a common culture

extremism political or religious movement that calls for extreme or radical solutions, often with no compromise

horde federation of nomadic tribes

International Atomic Energy Agency (IAEA) UN agency responsible for monitoring the use and spread of nuclear material around the world

Mongol related to the main population of Mongolia

Muslims followers of the religion of Islam

nomads members of a tribe or people that has no permanent home and that travels from place to place in search of food or pasture

Organization for Security and Cooperation in Europe (OSCE) an international organization of fifty-five states from Europe, the Mediterranean, the Caucasus, Central Asia, and North America concerned with early warning for nuclear issues, conflict prevention, crisis management, and post-conflict rehabilitation in their regions

petroglyphs rock carvings, usually prehistoric

press journalists who report news through newspapers, magazines, radio, television, and the Internet

referendum submission of a law or a proposal to the direct vote of a people

Romanov the name of the ruling family of the Russian Empire from 1613 to 1917

Russian Soviet Federated Socialist Republic (RSFSR) established in 1917, it was the largest of the Soviet republics and became modern-day Russia in 1991

shamanism religion based on a belief in good and evil spirits who can be influenced only by religious leaders called shamans

sharia the sacred law of Islam, embracing all aspects of a Muslim's life

Soviet Union formally named the **Union of Soviet Socialist Republics (USSR)** a former country established in 1922 with the RSFSR and other Soviet republics

steppes flat, dry grasslands of Europe and Asia

telecommunications communication by electronic or electric means

Turkic family of languages that includes Turkish, Azerbaijani, Tatar, Uighur, Uzbek, and Kazakh

United Nations (UN) an international organization founded in 1945 to promote peace, security, and economic development around the world

For More Information

Books

Ingram, Scott. *Joseph Stalin*. Woodbridge, CT: Blackbirch Press, 2002.

Furgus, Michael, and Janar Jandosova, eds. *Kazakhstan: Coming of Age*. London, England: Stacey International Publishers, 2004.

Major, John S. *Caravan to America: Learning Arts of the Silk Road*. Washington, DC: Smithsonian Center for Folklife and Cultural Heritage, 2002.

Mesh, Sally, Stanley Mesh, and Bruce McAllister. *You've Got Mail from Kazakhstan*. Higganum, CT: Higganum Hill Books, 2003.

Rice, Earle. *Empire of the East: The Story of Genghis Khan*. Greensboro, NC: Morgan Reynolds, 2005.

Tay, Alan. *Welcome to Kazakhstan*. Milwaukee: Gareth Stevens, 2005.

Web Sites

plasma.nationalgeographic.com/mapmachine/profiles/kz.html
Maps and information about Kazakhstan from National Geographic.

www.homestead.com/prosites-kazakhembus/sayitinkazakh.html
How to speak in Kazakh.

www.kazakinfo.com/
Site that specializes in all kinds of information about Kazakhstan.

www.state.gov/r/pa/ei/bgn/5487.htm
The most up-to-date information about Kazakhstan from the U.S. Department of State Fact Book.

Index

About the Author

Charles Piddock is a former editor in chief of Weekly Reader Corporation, publisher of sixteen classroom magazines for schools from pre-K through high school, including *Current Events, Current Science,* and *Teen Newsweek.* In his career with Weekly Reader, he has written and edited hundreds of articles for young people of all ages on world and national affairs, science, literature, and other topics. Before working at Weekly Reader, he worked in publishing in New York City and, before that, served as a Peace Corps volunteer in rural West Bengal, India.